Invitations

from

God

Barbara DeStefano, OSF

Mary Ann Warner
327 MAC Ave
East Lansing, MI 48823

The Center for Learning

The Author Barbara DeStefano , OSF, a member of the School Sisters of St. Francis from the Bethlehem Province, has been serving on the retreat team at the St. Francis Center for Renewal for the last thirteen years. Prior to her retreat work, Barbara taught both elementary and high school. A native Philadelphian, she earned her B.A. in theology at St. Joseph University, and obtained her M.A. in Religious Studies from St. Charles Seminary in Philadelphia.

The Publishing Team Rose Schaffer, HM, M.A., President/Chief Executive Officer
Bernadette Vetter, HM, M.A., Vice President
Donna Emerson, CSJ, M.A., Coordinator of Parish Publications

Art Direction Krina K. Walsh, B.S.I.D.

Photography Krina K. Walsh, B.S.I.D.

Nihil Obstat The Reverend George Smiga, S.T.D., MDiv.
Censor Deputatis

Imprimatur The Most Reverend Anthony M. Pilla, D.D., M.A.
Bishop of Cleveland

February 4, 1995

Contents

	Page
Introduction	v

Part I—Listening to Creation

Waking Up	3
This Flower	6
Ode to Light and Darkness	9
Old Zacchaeus's Farewell	14
Mother Earth, Birthing Womb	17
Seasons Lived, Seasons Remembered	21

Part II—Walking the Inner Journey

Sing a New Song	29
Reflections of a Sheep	34
Jerusalem	37
Wolf of Gubbio	41
To Peace	45
The Edge	47
Simon Peter Returns	50
Autumn Lessons from a Midnight Friend	56
Rediscovering My Heart	61

Part III—Living the Paschal Mystery

Beatitudes Alive	65
Hope Restored	68
Tent People	70
Women of God	72
A Toast	76
Called to Servanthood	80
The Circle of Life	82
Abba, Father	85
Transfigured God	88
Who Do You Say That I Am?	92

Introduction

The journey can be ever so ordinary, ever so routine. In the midst of our daily routine, however, there are special times when a touch of joy gleams from the eye's window—times like taking a leisurely walk on a spring day, feeling the union of souls in a moment shared with a friend, or recapturing one's own initial innocence in the face of a child.

If we see these surprise memos from our Creator God as holy invitations, as a loving lure into divine intimacy, as *the Scriptural call*; in a sense, to "remove our shoes before this burning bush," unimagined miracles can happen in the unexpecting soul.

The reflections shared in this book hopefully prompt responses to these unexplainable encounters. Words never really "measure up" to the reality of the spiritual realm. Nevertheless, when they seem to arise from the depth of one's inner being, where the Spirit cries "Abba," they hold an impelling force that urges one to share.

This book is everyone's journey with God on ordinary and extraordinary days. There are three sections: Listening to Creation, Walking the Inner Journey, and Living the Paschal Mystery. Each section has a series of poems. After each poem, there are suggestions for scripture reading(s) and prayer and journal space to write one's reflection.

May this journey remind us that we are brothers and sisters who stand as ONE before our creative, loving, inviting God.

Dedication

Dedicated to my Mom, Rose (DeStefano) Horn,
whose love and nurturing, since the moment of
my conception, have given birth and freedom
to the poetry that sings its music in my soul.

Part I—

Listening

to Creation

Waking Up

Morning!
The grace of wakefulness!
The knowledge of night-time care!
The belief that
    as the body sleeps,
    the soul continues its rendezvous
    with its God!
The conviction that
    as the body takes its rest,
    the spirit,
    uninhibited by defenses,
    communes with the Holy Spirit,
    its very life and breath!
All of these
    call us from the solitude
    of our inner fortresses.

    Morning freshness!
    Morning newness!
    Morning beauty!
    They entice us.
    They lure us
        into creativity and relationship
        with the world alive with consciousness
        with life around us
        simmering with sacred energy.
            This new day is holy.
            This day is the priesthood of Melchizedek,
                the ladder of Jacob,
                the holy ground of Moses,
                the anointing of David.
            It is the command given to Abraham
                to leave,
                to move to a new land.

        This new day is sacramental,
            touched with the presence of God,
            full of miracles,
                like the Sea of Reeds,
                like the dry bones of Ezekiel,
                like the pool of Siloam,
                like the new vision in Jericho,
                like the very cloak of Jesus,
                the one that healed a woman
                    of great faith.

This new day is pregnant with possibilities.
It is full of grace—like Mary.
It is grounded in history.
It roots us in the communion of saints,
 and sets us asail
 on our own Sea of Galilee
 to travel with our Master and LORD.
  What can we say?
  How do we respond
   to such grace and power?
  What stance could be fitting
   in the face of such holiness and majesty?—
   except . . .
   to fall on our knees
   and chant our morning praise,
   and then,
   feast on the "daily bread"
   that God gives.

Journal Suggestion

Try rising before sunrise. Pray this poem/prayer. Greet the day with a song of praise that is meaningful to you. Spend some quiet time afterwards. Read and reflect on the scripture passage below from *Isaiah 60:1-6.* As the experience "sinks in,"—so to speak— perhaps walk outside or sit in your favorite prayer space. Journal your reaction. Is there a difference in how you are approaching *this* morning as compared with other mornings? Choose a symbol to carry with you through the day—*e.g.,* a flower from the garden, a small twig from a tree, a picture of a sunrise. . . .

Scripture Reading

Isaiah 60:1–6

Glory of the New Zion

Rise up in splendor! Your light has come,
    the glory of the Lord shines upon you.
See, darkness covers the earth,
    and thick clouds cover the peoples;
But upon you the Lord shines,
    and over you appears his glory.
Nations shall walk by your light,
    and kings by your shining radiance.
Raise your eyes and look about;
    they all gather and come to you:
Your sons come from afar,
    and your daughters in the arms of their
        nurses.

Then you shall be radiant at what you see,
    your heart shall throb and overflow,
For the riches of the sea shall be emptied
        out before you,
    the wealth of nations shall be brought to
        you.
Caravans of camels shall fill you,
    dromedaries from Midian and Ephah;
All from Sheba shall come
    bearing gold and frankincense,
    and proclaiming the praises of the Lord.

Your Journal Space

This Flower

This flower—
its own unique beauty,
its petal freshness,
its Creator-life,
its colored array all its own,
its earth-green leaves
expressive of its nature-kinship!

This flower—
full of God,
full of grace-potential
to brighten darkness
and decorate emptiness,
to lift up hearts
and plant more seeds!

This flower—
beautiful in My sight
in all its simplicity,
in its aloneness,
its sacrificing its life
for the sake of My people!

This flower
is the "apple of My eye."
I love it
with an affection
beyond its imagining.
It has had a place in my heart
even as a seed
not yet planted.

Hold your flower
gently, but protectively
in your hand.
Draw it close to your heart.
It has something to tell you.
It speaks heart-words!

It will tell you
what a beautiful flower YOU are!
It will show you
the indescribable love
with which I planted YOU.

Did you know that
the planting,
the caring,
even the sowing
were different
for each of you?

You are so precious to Me.
Give me your heart.
Be the flower
you were destined to be.
Be my flower.
And know that
all of My people,
all of your sisters and brothers,
are flowers to Me.
They need to know—
Tell them!

Journal Suggestion

Read *Isaiah 43:1-7*. Slowly read the poem. Do you really believe in God's personal love for you? How have you experienced it in your life? Is there a part of you, a part of your life, your past, that you have difficulty loving? Speak to Jesus about it. Write your reflection in the journal space.

Scripture Reading

Isaiah 43:1–7

Chapter 43
Promises of Redemption and Restoration

But now, thus says the LORD,
> who created you, O Jacob, and formed
> you, O Israel:
Fear not, for I have redeemed you;
> I have called you by name: you are mine.
When you pass through the water, I will be
> with you;
> in the rivers you shall not drown.
When you walk through fire, you shall not
> be burned;
> the flames shall not consume you.
For I am the LORD, your God,
> the Holy One of Israel, your savior.
I give Egypt as your ransom,
> Ethiopia and Seba in return for you.
Because you are precious in my eyes
> and glorious, and because I love you.
I give men in return for you
> and peoples in exchange for your life.
Fear not, for I am with you;
> from the east I will bring back your
> descendants,
> from the west I will gather you.
I will say to the north: Give them up!
> and to the south: Hold not back!
Bring back my sons from afar,
> and my daughters from the ends of the
> earth:
Everyone who is named as mine,
> whom I created for my glory,
> whom I formed and made.

Your Journal Space

Ode to Light and Darkness

The sun has set.
It's warming, massaging rays
no longer shine
through my pleading window—
gently soothing all in its path.
Its light no longer wakes the sleeping,
nor reveals what was hidden
under cover of the dark.
Its brightness,
signifying all goodness and holiness,
even Divinity Itself,
has yielded to the peace
of night's solace.
Brother Sun has finished
his work here for today,
and moves on to awaken
our brothers and sisters
in another place.
He ministers to all
of Mother Earth's children.
I look outside.
I can see that the trees
continue to breathe with life,
and dance with Brother Wind.
They do not fight
the rhythm cycle
of day/night timing,
nor cringe with fear
in the darkness.
In fact,
they appear to make
their OWN kind of light.
You see, the sun has left them
a part of himself
and their open hearts
received him well.

I, too, feel a presence
in my heart.
Is it Brother Sun, dwelling there?—
making it forever daylight
in my soul?
Brother Sun,
my Brother,
Son of God,
Jesus,
transfigured again and again
in the depths of my being—
gently molding
and remolding
my sinful tendencies.
God's light, God's grace,
the very life of the Trinitarian God
that we worship with awe
fills me,
penetrates my every cell,
and transforms me
into God's image and likeness.

When I look out my window
in the darkness of evening,
I do not fear its darkness.
I do not hide from its loneliness.
I have learned how to listen
to the Voice calling from deep
within,
"Come and see!" it seems to say,
as it sees my soul groping
to see where the Master stays.

The window in my room
is my friend,
a non-threatening, inviting friend,
that teaches me about life
and her emptiness.
All I have to do
is sit beside this rabbi,
and look out with quietness
of mind and soul.
But its wisdom pales
next to Jesus,
the Teacher "par excellence."
Do I dare to look within—
to see the kingdom of God
and to learn
of the deeper mysteries
of another sacred realm?

The sun has set.
Its warming, massaging rays
no longer shine
through my pleading window.
But look!
Another light
has taken its position
on the cosmic stage
of life's drama.
Sister Moon looks down on me
from her place among the stars.
She seems to know me,
like a mother who has not forgotten
the child in her womb.
She calls me by name
and tells me of her love
and how precious I am to her.
This moon fills me with HOPE,
not only with the joyful anticipation
that a new day is coming,
but with the heartfelt confidence that
even the darkest of nights
is much brighter
than we will ever know.
PRAISE YOU, MY LORD,
FOR BROTHER SUN AND SISTER
MOON.

Journal Suggestion

Read and reflect on *Psalm 27* and *John 8:12*. Reread the poem.
Gently recall the times of light and the times of darkness in your
life. Spend prayer time on each light/darkness phase of experience.
On looking back now, can you see that some good has come out
of each one? Journal first your prayers of thanks for the good
experiences or fruits. Then, also write about any areas that still
need healing.

Scripture Readings

Psalm 27

A

I

The Lord is my light and my salvation;
> whom do I fear?

The Lord is my life's refuge;
> of whom am I afraid?

When evildoers come at me
> to devour my flesh,

These my enemies and foes
> themselves stumble and fall.

Though an army encamp against me,
> my heart does not fear;

Though war be waged against me,
> even then do I trust.

II

One thing I ask of the Lord;
> this I seek:

To dwell in the Lord's house
> all the days of my life,

To gaze on the Lord's beauty,
> to visit his temple.

For God will hide me in his shelter
> in time of trouble,

Will conceal me in the cover of his tent;
> and set me high upon a rock.

Even now my head is held high
> above my enemies on every side!

I will offer in his tent
> sacrifices with shouts of joy;
>> I will sing and chant praise to the Lord.

B

I

Hear my voice, LORD, when I call;
    have mercy on me and answer me.
"Come," says my heart,"seek God's face";
    your face, LORD, do I seek!
Do not hide your face from me;
    do not repel your servant in anger.
You are my help; do not cast me off;
    do not forsake me, God my savior!
Even if my father and mother forsake me,
    the LORD will take me in.

II

LORD, show me your way;
    lead me on a level path
    because of my enemies.
Do not abandon me to the will of my foes;
    malicious and lying witnesses have risen
        against me.
But I believe I shall enjoy the LORD's
        goodness
    in the land of the living.
Wait for the LORD, take courage;
    be stouthearted, wait for the LORD!

John 8:12

Jesus spoke to them again, saying, "I am the light of the world.
Whoever follows me will not walk in darkness, but will have
the light of life."

Your Journal Space

Old Zacchaeus's Farewell

My friend,
I will be leaving you soon.
Old age has made its gentle, almost unnoticeable, appearance in my life
and my days are numbered.
How precious you have become to me!
You, the Source of the most treasured grace in my life!

O Tree,
I knew you since the time of my youth.
I had passed by you countless times on the road.
I had hid behind your trunk in playfulness with my friends.
I had climbed up your varied branches
to enjoy your company,
when no one else had time for me.
At the time,
you seemed like any other sycamore.

Then, one day, Jesus touched our lives.
Little did I know long ago
that I would share this moment with you.
Do you remember it as vividly, as tenderly, as I do?
The Master was preaching in our town.
All I had dared to hope for
was to get a mere glimpse of him above the crowds.
As you had done so often before,
you held me up
with the strength of your trunk,
and the depth of your roots.

When I think
of how he looked at me,
of the sacrament of our eyes meeting,
of the music of the Shepherd's voice calling MY name,
my heart still dances with a joy,
that has been born in a changed soul.
Yes, my sycamore friend,
just being with you brings back that moment.

Thank you for always being there for me,
for being my very own symbol,
reminding me every day
where I met the LORD.
Since that day of grace,
you have always had my friendship and affection.

I bid you farewell, my life companion!
I will miss you.
You, too, have grown old.
Rest now.
You have done your work,
as life-giver, as evangelizer.
Now, you will sing of the LORD,
by your very presence.

Journal Suggestion

Begin with a reflective reading of *Luke 19:1–10*. Take time to recall a "sycamore tree" experience in YOUR life—*i.e.*, a time, event, or a personal experience that was a significant encounter with your God. Spend time just "sitting with" the memory. With the added grace of being able to see more clearly in retrospect, journal a prayer of thanksgiving for the blessings received then.

Is there a symbol you can choose to remind you of this moment in your personal history, as the tree had become a symbol for Zacchaeus? Keep that symbol someplace visible over these next weeks.

Scripture Reading

Luke 19:1–10

Zacchaeus the Tax Collector
He came to Jericho and intended to pass through the town. Now a man there named Zacchaeus, who was a chief tax collector and also a wealthy man, was seeking to see who Jesus was; but he could not see him because of the crowd, for he was short in stature. So he ran ahead and climbed a sycamore tree in order to see Jesus, who was about to pass that way. When he reached the place, Jesus looked up and said to him, "Zacchaeus, come down quickly, for today I must stay at your house." And he came down quickly and received him with joy. When they all saw this, they began to grumble, saying, "He has gone to stay at the house of a sinner." But Zacchaeus stood there and said to the Lord, "Behold, half of my possessions, Lord, I shall give to the poor, and if I have extorted anything from anyone I shall repay it four times over." And Jesus said to him, "Today salvation has come to this house because this man too is a descendant of Abraham. For the Son of Man has come to seek and to save what was lost."

Your Journal Space

Mother Earth, Birthing Womb

All praise be Yours, my LORD, through Sister Earth, our Mother,
    Who feeds us in her sovereignty and produces
    Various fruits, with flowers and herbs.

Like all mothers, Earth has a way
    of giving of herself
    and receiving what is given her.
She shares life with all who look to her
    with all who tread on her soil
    and eat of her fruits.
Earth is open, receptive, trusting, and vulnerable.
She receives the seed that falls to her and dies.
She nurses the dying seed,
    holds it in her arms
    close to her heart.
She gives it care, puts it to rest,
    and keeps vigil at its bedside.
And when the seed breathes its final breath,
    and Sister Death comes for it,
    Mother Earth does not mourn.
She feels no grief—nor fear, nor loss.
For the seed lives in her heart
    and has impregnated her life-giving womb.

Once again, as has happened countless times,
God, her Creator and LORD,
    has commissioned her.
He has called her by name.
She listens to the voice coming from within
    and reverently responds, "Here I am, LORD,"
    for she knows that she lives in holy space,
    and she herself is holy ground.
Earth's mission is to give what she has been given,
    to bring forth the seed-life of her soul,
    to birth it into life again
        with reverence for the presence of grace,
    to cradle it
        with the love and affection
        of a woman for the child of her womb.
She is like the sower of all seed,
    scattering the seeds throughout history,
    bearing fruit and colorful flowers along the way.

Some turn away from this new life.
They are frightened of change
    and prefer the security,
    even if it means remaining stagnant.
Some accept it ever so politely,
    graciously,
    even gratefully,
    then cast it aside
    as useless to the pragmatic, scientific, sophisticated mind.
Some fail to see the gift at all—
    their eyes blinded by other cares and interests.

Some, however, stand out in history—
    indeed—throughout **our** history,
    as seed-bearers and seed-sharers:
    our sisters and brothers from our line of spiritual ancestry
    who knew that the seed must die
        in the soil of Mother Earth,
    who were not afraid of Sister Death,
    who believed in the depths of their hearts
        that soil, made fertile by the breath of the Spirit,
        gives new life.
They received the seed
    and it yielded a rich harvest:
    Abraham and Sarah,
    Isaac, Jacob, Moses,
    Zachary and Elizabeth,
    Mary of Nazareth,
    Simon Peter,
    James and John,
    Mary of Magdala,
    Lazarus,
    Mary and Martha of Bethany.

It is in these receptive hearts
    that we, the followers of Jesus,
    find our identity and our calling,
    living and growing in all times and places,
    listening for the divine voice in our own seed hearts,
    blessed by the sower's grace
        dwelling within and around us,
    grateful to Mother Earth,
        to Sister Death,
        and to the most high God.

We are all sisters and brothers—
    all of us—
    playing before Creator God.
All of us—
    our foremothers and forefathers—
    and we
    live on the same Earth,
    walk on the same ground,
    breathe in the same air,
    worship the same God,
    and share the same call.
Our unity transcends time and place.
"Unless the seed falls to the ground and dies,
    it remains only a seed."

The seed of our Church,
    rooted in Jesus,
    continuing among the Jewish people
        by Peter, James, and the other apostles,
    blossoming further to the Gentiles
        by Paul and Barnabas,
    kept alive in the homes by our spiritual ancestors,
    has entered fully into the paschal mystery of Jesus—
        dying and rising in varied ways,
        under many circumstances,
        and lives on today in **our** souls, in **our** lives.

All praise be Yours, my LORD, through Sister Earth, our Mother,
    Who feeds us in her sovereignty and produces
    Various fruits, with flowers and herbs.

Journal Suggestion

Reflect on *John 12:23–25*. The earth and its relationship to the
seed that "falls to the earth and dies" have become symbols for the
Church's dying/rising cycle. Spend some time with Mother Earth.
What lessons has she to teach you about your history?...about your
life now? Evaluate your own relationship to Mother Earth. Has
your treatment of her been one of reverence and gratitude?

Scripture Reading

John 12:23–24

Jesus answered them, "The hour has come for the Son of Man to be glorified. Amen, amen, I say to you, unless a grain of wheat falls to the ground and dies, it remains just a grain of wheat; but if it dies, it produces much fruit.

Your Journal Space

Seasons Lived,
Seasons Remembered

Our lives are in God's hands.
So is the life of our family,
...our Church.

All things have their seasons
—their winters of barrenness,
—their springs of new buddings,
—their summers of warm flowerings,
—their autumns of slow sheddings.
So does our world.

To everything there is a season:
a time for beginnings,
and a time for endings...
beginnings in childhood,
beginnings in adulthood,
beginnings in mid-life,
beginnings in later years.

Every stage of our growth
has been a new beginning.

Every newborn dream,
every problem solved, every endeavor tried,
every challenge faced, every question raised—
all new steps on our common journey
of heart and soul, spirit and dream.

Each new generation
and each renewed old one
have taken brand new steps
in brand new shoes
to meet the callings of their time and season.

For them and for us,
there were times of joy and sorrow,
there were times of building faith in each other
and struggling together through the doubts we felt.

There were times of fun and laughter,
hopes envisioned and celebrations shared.
There were also conflicts and grievings,
hurts and reconciliations—all essential parts of
human life lived and shared
through the seasons of time.

There were endings too...
endings caused by the
limitations of time,
by the human condition,
and by new invitations
of the Spirit of God;

endings that frighten us
with their disguise of finality,
when all the while they know
that new beginnings await us
on the other side;

endings like
the loss of a job,
a broken friendship,
separation from people we love,
the end of a marriage,
the death of a loved one,
children moving on—
and moving out.

All seasons of time come to an end,
but only so that a new birth in time
can take place and bear fruit.
"If I do not leave you,
the Paraclete will not come."

Oh, if Spirit-life is to breathe in us,
as it once breathed in the depths
of our ancestors,
of the Communion of Saints,
then we must accept endings well—
with courage and graciousness,
with affection and even eagerness,
because we know in deep faith,
that a new door is waiting
to be opened.

"With the one that opens the door,
I will sit and have supper."

Yes, to everything there is a season.
Time, we do not always understand you.
It seems, at times, that your steps are
too quick and without feeling.
And we try to escape you or hold you back.

Forgive us for not respecting your wisdom
and clarity of perception.
Accept our commitment of trust and loyalty.
We will journey with you;
we will learn to keep pace with you,
even though we do not know where
you may be leading us.

We give ourselves to you.
We give each other to you—
with full confidence in Your obedience
to the Spirit of God,
the God Who created even you,
the God to Whom even you must bow.

May this God of all times and all seasons
bless us and guide us,
during times of prosperity
and times of hardship,
during times of constancy
and times of change.

May the God of our foremothers
and forefathers,
the God of the leaders, and prophets,
and saints of old,
the God of seasons lived
and seasons remembered,
be the God of peace and wisdom,
who will reign in our hearts—
indeed, in **all** hearts.

Journal Suggestion

Begin with the praying of *Psalm 139*, and conclude your prayer time by reading *Ecclesiastes 3:1–8*. Divide your life journey this far into seasons—significant beginnings and endings, times of major decisions, of losses, of grievings, of important changes. Take time with each season and "Pray it." If feelings emerge, acknowledge them and write them down. If there are still unhealed areas—ask God to touch and transform them. Give thanks for the presence of God through all the seasons of your life.

Scripture Readings

Psalm 139

I
LORD, you have probed me, you know me:
    you know when I sit and stand;
    you understand my thoughts from afar.
My travels and my rest you mark;
    with all my ways you are familiar.
Even before a word is on my tongue,
    LORD, you know it all.
Behind and before you encircle me
    and rest your hand upon me.
Such knowledge is beyond me,
    far too lofty for me to reach.

II
Where can I hide from your spirit?
    From your presence, where can I flee?
If I ascend to the heavens, you are there;
    if I lie down in Sheol, you are there too.
If I fly with the wings of dawn
    and alight beyond the sea,
Even there your hand will guide me,
    your right hand hold me fast.
If I say, "Surely darkness shall hide me,
    and night shall be my light"—
Darkness is not dark for you,
    and night shines as the day.
    Darkness and light are but one.

III
You formed my inmost being;
    you knit me in my mother's womb.
I praise you, so wonderfully you made me;
    wonderful are your works!
My very self you knew;
    my bones were not hidden from you,
When I was being made in secret,
    fashioned as in the depths of the earth.
Your eyes foresaw my actions;
    in your book all are written down;
    my days were shaped, before one came to
        be.

IV
How precious to me are your designs, O
        God;
    how vast the sum of them!
Were I to count, they would outnumber the
        sands;
    to finish, I would need eternity.
If only you would destroy the wicked, O
        God,
    and the bloodthirsty would depart from
        me!
Deceitfully they invoke your name;
    your foes swear faithless oaths.
Do I not hate, Lord, those who hate you?
    Those who rise against you, do I not
        loathe?
With fierce hatred I hate them,
    enemies I count as my own.

V
Probe me, God, know my heart;
    try me, know my concerns.
See if my way is crooked,
    then lead me in the ancient paths.

There is an appointed time for everything,
    and a time for every affair under the
        heavens.
A time to be born, and a time to die;
    a time to plant, and a time to uproot the
        plant.
A time to kill, and a time to heal;
    a time to tear down, and a time to build.
A time to weep, and a time to laugh;
    a time to mourn, and a time to dance.
A time to scatter stones, and a time to
        gather them;
    a time to embrace, and a time to be far
        from embraces.
A time to seek, and a time to lose;
    a time to keep, and a time to cast away.
A time to rend, and a time to sew;
    a time to be silent, and a time to speak.
A time to love, and a time to hate;
    a time of war, and a time of peace.

Your Journal Space

Part II

Walking the
Inner Journey

Sing a New Song

Inside of us—
somewhere—
at a level where only God knows us,
there is a song waiting to be sung.
Its melody has been born
from the unique experiences
that have touched us
since the moment of conception.
Note by note our song has developed—
each one recounting
every minute lived,
every breath taken,
every heartbeat recorded
in Life's journal.

Life leaves her messages
deep in our center—
both her gifts,
all wrapped in warming, playful colors,
and her scars,
yearning for healing and freedom.
Entire symphonies,
overflowing with drama and emotion,
await their time
of expression and communing.
They believe;
they **know**,
their time will come.
And they practice their future performance
with great respect
for divine timing.

The key signature
may differ for each person.
It includes one's whole history,
one's unique identity,
and one's personal dreams
instilled in the heart
by the Holy Spirit.
But, the rhythm and the tempo
are the same for all;
for, we must follow
the rhythm of Life herself.

In entrusting our feelings
and perceptions to Life,
we find she will prepare us
to keep the rhythm
already set before time began,
the rhythm to which
the whole cosmos has been dancing
for all eternity.

This song within lives on
and, at certain times,
it seems to take on a newness.
It is affected
by the surprises that come its way,
by the harmonies
that emerge and embellish it
and transform its voice,
by the chords and countermelodies
that add more beauty
and greater intensity
to this masterpiece.
Sometimes,
if we listen attentively in the silence,
we can hear the instruments
tuning for the opera
to which our souls will give birth.
We can even see the dancers,
donned in their ballet slippers,
taking their places backstage.

It is at those moments
when all of life seems to stand still,
that we sense the oneness of God's creation.
The center of all living things
focuses itself
on the Master Conductor, Jesus Christ who calls us
to sing a new song.
His life
has counted out the measures.
His death
has edited our clashes
and discordant tones.
His Resurrection
has made our songs
new and different,
strong with conviction
yet gentle,
filled with grace.

So sing,
my brothers and sisters!
Sing your song to the LORD!
Let your spirits run free!
Do not be afraid.
There is no proper method.
Whatever you play
will be heard with love.
The music you make
will blend in
with the music all around you.
And it will give life to the lyrics
that will be drawn to the Word
with the magnetic resonance
of the universe.
Don't hold back!
Yield to the power of your God
and the urging voice of the Spirit.
It is this Spirit
that plays its melody in your soul.
Sing a new song to the LORD.
Sing a new song.

Journal Suggestion

Begin by reading *Psalm 98, Ephesians 5:1-2, 15-20*. Try composing your own song. Let it come from your heart, that sacred space where God dwells. Don't worry about such matters as rhyme or rhythm. This is between you and God.

The psalms that have come down to us from the time of David were also sung. They were "song-prayers." Perhaps, you may find it easier to write your own psalm. It is helpful to begin with one of the Old Testament psalms—perhaps, the one on the next page— or any that fit the mood of your prayer. Write part of the psalm. Then, continue in your own words.

Scripture Readings

Psalm 98

The Coming of God

I

Sing a new song to the LORD,
 who has done marvelous deeds,
Whose right hand and holy arm
 have won the victory.
The LORD has made his victory known;
 has revealed his triumph for the
  nations to see,
Has remembered faithful love
 toward the house of Israel.
All the ends of the earth have seen
 the victory of our God.

II

Shout with joy to the LORD, all the earth;
 break into song; sing praise.
Sing praise to the LORD with the harp,
 with the harp and melodious song.
With trumpets and the sound of the horn
 shout with joy to the King, the LORD.

III

Let the sea and what fills it resound,
 the world and those who dwell there.
Let the rivers clap their hands,
 the mountains shout with them for
  joy,
Before the LORD who comes,
 who comes to govern the earth,
To govern the world with justice
 and the peoples with fairness.

Ephesians 5:1–2, 15–20

So be imitators of God, as beloved children, and live in love, as Christ loved us and handed himself over for us as a sacrificial offering to God for a fragrant aroma.

Watch carefully then how you live, not as foolish persons but as wise, making the most of the opportunity, because the days are evil. Therefore, do not continue in ignorance, but try to understand what is the will of the Lord. And do not get drunk on wine, in which lies debauchery, but be filled with the Spirit, addressing one another [in] psalms and hymns and spiritual songs, singing and playing to the Lord in your hearts, giving thanks always and for everything in the name of our Lord Jesus Christ to God the Father.

Your Journal Space

Reflections of a Sheep

I am a sheep,
just one in a flock of many,
a small sheep compared to the others,
sometimes overlooked,
sometimes forgotten,
with no outstanding mark of uniqueness.

I am a sheep.
I feel lost and frightened, at times,
foolish and insignificant, at others.
Many sheep are stronger than I;
their coat, fuller,
their senses, keener.

I am a sheep.
My sheep's brain, simple and poor,
leads me to wander aimlessly.
I blindly follow the others—
not knowing where they go.
And when I stray,
I am more foolish, indeed.

My sheep's feet stumble and trip.
There is no grace in my gait,
no firmness in my step.

My sheep's body is clumsy and awkward.
I have seen now and again
a fawn leaping gracefully through the fields,
or an eagle flying freely in the limitless sky,
and I feel envy.
but I trudge along with what I have.

My sheep's wool is dirty and thick.
It is tangled and matted,
unlike the silky skins of other animals.

Yes, I am a sheep through and through,
but, I am happy still and all,
because I have a Shepherd
who knows me even amidst
the ninety-nine others in the flock,
a Shepherd who has given me
significance and dignity by his loving care.

This Shepherd calls me back when I wander,
feeds me abundantly in green pastures,
guides me tenderly to cool waters.

Simple though I am,
stumbling though I do,
awkward though I look,
this Shepherd looks upon me
with eyes of tenderness,
with a heart-sight,
with love and even with pride
in the creation of God that He sees.

How else could I feel,
except joyful in my lowly sheep's heart?
"Who am I?" I say to myself,
"That God should care for me?
Who am I?"

Journal Suggestion

Begin your prayer time by reading *John 10:7–16*. Imagine for a
while your being there during Jesus' teaching about the relationship
between the Shepherd and the sheep. How does it feel to hear Jesus
tell you that he knows you, that he calls you by name, that Jesus
has come that you may have life, that Jesus will lay down his life
for you? Imagine that, after the crowds leave, you stay behind with
Jesus. Nothing else is said. You sit next to Jesus and rest your head
on him. Whenever you are ready, record your feelings. Tell Jesus
how you feel in a closing prayer. Write it in the Journal Space.

Scripture Reading

John 10:7–16

So Jesus said again, "Amen, amen, I say to you, I am the gate for the sheep. All who came [before me] are thieves and robbers, but the sheep did not listen to them. I am the gate. Whoever enters through me will be saved, and will come in and go out and find pasture. A thief comes only to steal and slaughter and destroy; I came so that they might have life and have it more abundantly. I am the good shepherd. A good shepherd lays down his life for the sheep. A hired man, who is not a shepherd and whose sheep are not his own, sees a wolf coming and leaves the sheep and runs away, and the wolf catches and scatters them. This is because he works for pay and has no concern for the sheep. I am the good shepherd, and I know mine and mine know me, just as the Father knows me and I know the Father; and I will lay down my life for the sheep. I have other sheep that do not belong to this fold. These also I must lead, and they will hear my voice, and there will be one flock, one shepherd.

Your Journal Space

Jerusalem

Jerusalem,
City of God.
Dwelling place
of the Ark of the Covenant,
City of holiness,
of mountain greatness,
of miracle power,
and temple glory,
City that calls together
God's people,
City that addresses their soul
and bids them
to remove their shoes.

Jerusalem,
House of holiness,
House of wisdom,
Strength in meekness,
Defeated in history
yet, standing still
firm on Messianic rock,
cornerstone roots

Babylonian violence,
Roman destruction
charging through the city walls
with tornado force.
Walls torn down,
Houses set afire,
Human lives taken
yet, with nothing left
but heart.
The city lives on,
pulsating with life,
Yahweh's promise,
Life without end,
The real temple inside—
inside believers—
inside their communion
with one another,
A sanctuary of the Holy of Holies
that will never die.

Jerusalem,
Centuries later
Touched by Jesus.
His footsteps made sacred
the soil of her land.
His words resounded in her air
blessing it as it moved on its way.
His hours of rest on rock or hill
forever gave dignity
to the earth beneath him.
Wonders abounded
as Jesus walked among his people:
Water transformed into wine
Sight given to blinded eyes.
An angry sea calmed
by a greater Power,
An untouchable cured
and touched.
Healing energy released
from a mere garment's hem.

Jerusalem
Holy ground
Place of salvation
City of Crucifixion-blood
Proclaimer of Resurrection-glory
Memories of Servant's Foot-washing
Table of Eucharist
Promise of Presence
Commandment of love
Forgiveness-gift
Spirit-life.

Jerusalem,
City of God
Dwelling Place of Jesus
Church community
My sisters and brothers,
I praise You
I recognize in you
the sanctuary of the Most High
And I fall on bended knee
at the mention of Your name.

Journal Suggestion

There are several Scripture texts that refer to the City of God. *Psalm 122* expresses the joy of God's people at being able to return home after the exile. *Revelations 21:1–7* gives the eschatological look at the "new Jerusalem."

Find the parallels between your own life journey and the journey of Jerusalem. When were your moments of glory and strength? When were the struggles, the internal wars, the oppression from the outside? Can you recall some sacred moments when you were conscious of the temple inside of you? How have the footsteps of Jesus made you "holy ground" where Eucharist is empowered to deepen and grow?

Scripture Readings

Psalm 122
A Pilgrim's Prayer for Jerusalem
1 A song of ascents. Of David.

I
I rejoiced when they said to me,
    "Let us go to the house of the LORD."
And now our feet are standing
    within your gates, Jerusalem.
Jerusalem, built as a city,
    walled round about.
Here the tribes have come,
    the tribes of the LORD,
As it was decreed for Israel,
    to give thanks to the name of the LORD.
Here are the thrones of justice,
    the thrones of the house of David.

II
For the peace of Jerusalem pray:
    "May those who love you prosper!
May peace be within your ramparts,
    prosperity within your towers."
For family and friends I say,
    "May peace be yours."
For the house of the LORD, our God, I pray,
    "May blessings be yours."

The New Heaven and the New Earth

Then I saw a new heaven and a new earth. The former heaven and the former earth had passed away, and the sea was no more. I also saw the holy city, a new Jerusalem, coming down out of heaven from God, prepared as a bride adorned for her husband. I heard a loud voice from the throne saying, "Behold, God's dwelling is with the human race. He will dwell with them and they will be his people and God himself will always be with them [as their God]. He will wipe every tear from their eyes, and there shall be no more death or mourning, wailing or pain, [for] the old order has passed away."

The one who sat on the throne said, "Behold, I make all things new." Then he said, "Write these words down, for they are trustworthy and true." He said to me, "They are accomplished. I [am] the Alpha and the Omega, the beginning and the end. To the thirsty I will give a gift from the spring of life-giving water. The victor will inherit these gifts, and I shall be his God, and he will be my son.

Your Journal Space

Wolf of Gubbio

*(A meditation response to the legend of St. Francis'
taming of the wolf in the town of Gubbio)*

Wolf of Gubbio,
do you live inside of me?
Aren't you that sometimes
overpowering part of me,
that huge and fierce part of me,
that unknown, unknowable part of me,
which I am afraid to face?
Jesus said the truth will set me free,
but, when I take my timid steps,
my "I'm-not-so-sure-I-want-to" steps,
to face you in truth,
I hear the Pilate in me,
philosophizing again:
"What is truth?"—
and my self-protection,
my self-deceit
feels justified.
People I love and who love me
have seen you in me.
They've even pointed you out.
But when I've dared to look,
the cutting sharpness of your teeth
and the ferociousness of your hunger
called forth the frightened Simon in me,
who said, "I do not know him."

      Wolf of Gubbio,
      do you live inside of me?
      Are you the one who lashes back
      when you have been hurt by another?
      Are you the one who has learned
      the art of tough disguise,
      so as not to be hurt again?
      Are you the one whose hunger to be fed
      is stronger at times
      than your ability to give food?

Come forward, Wolf of Gubbio!
Come and meet your brother, Francis.
You two have met before.
And the power of his LORD
has touched you,
has healed you.
Don't you remember?
God will reconcile us,
and integrate us,
so that we can walk the way of Jesus,
as did Francis.
We can walk side by side,
embracing each other as friends,
never again to deny each other's existence
or needs.

Wolf of Gubbio,
who lives inside of me,
all peace and goodness to you!

Journal Suggestion

For many of us, the greatest violence we encounter is the violence in our own hearts. Ask Jesus to teach you to recognize that violence, to name the forms it takes in you. Pray *Psalm 25* from a new perspective—as you view the "enemies that exult over you" as the ones within you. *Matthew 5:43-47* will remind you of Jesus' exhortation to love our enemies. In facing and embracing those aspects of ourselves that we try to deny, we allow the freedom of Jesus to dwell there and heal us. Try rewriting *Psalm 25* in your own words.

Scripture Readings

Psalm 25

Confident Prayer for Forgiveness and Guidance

1 Of David

I

I wait for you, O LORD;
 I lift up my soul
to my God.
In you I trust; do not let me be disgraced;
 do not let my enemies gloat over me.
No one is disgraced who waits for you,
 but only those who lightly break faith.
Make known to me your ways, LORD;
 teach me your paths.
Guide me in your truth and teach me,
 for you are God my savior.
For you I wait all the long day,
 because of your goodness, LORD.
Remember your compassion and love,
  O LORD;
 for they are ages old.
Remember no more the sins of my youth;
 remember me only in light of your love.

II

Good and upright is the LORD,
 who shows sinners the way,
Guides the humble rightly,
 and teaches the humble the way.
All the paths of the LORD are faithful love
  toward those who honor the covenant
   demands.
For the sake of your name, LORD,
 pardon my guilt, though it is great.
Who are those who fear the LORD?
 God shows them the way to choose.
They live well and prosper,
 and their descendants inherit the land.
The counsel of the LORD belongs to the
  faithful;
 the covenant instructs them.
My eyes are ever upon the LORD,
 who frees my feet from the snare.

III

Look upon me, have pity on me,
    for I am alone and afflicted.
Relieve the troubles of my heart
    bring me out of my distress.
Put an end to my affliction and suffering;
    take away all my sins.
See how many are my enemies,
    see how fiercely they hate me.
Preserve my life and rescue me;
    do not let me be disgraced, for I trust in
        you.
Let honesty and virtue preserve me;
    I wait for you, O LORD.
Redeem Israel, God,
    from all its distress!

Matthew 5:43–48

Love of Enemies

"You have heard that it was said, 'You shall love your neighbor and hate your enemy.' But I say to you, love your enemies, and pray for those who persecute you, that you may be children of your heavenly Father, for he makes his sun rise on the bad and the good, and causes rain to fall on the just and the unjust. For if you love those who love you, what recompense will you have? Do not the tax collectors do the same? And if you greet your brothers only, what is unusual about that? Do not the pagans do the same? So be perfect, just as your heavenly Father is perfect.

Your Journal Space

To Peace

In the depth of my heart
In the silence of my soul
In the midst of inner noise
In my struggles
In my prayer. . .
Peace, be my companion.

In my personal and family history
In my memories of past hurts
In my present living situation
In my hopes and in my dreams
In the stark reality of life
In my concept of self. . .
Peace, flow through me.

In the confusion that sometimes fills my mind
In the conflicts that are a part of relational living
In my necessary confrontations
In my need for healing
In my longing for wholeness. . .
Peace, soothe my soul.

In my good intentions and broken promises
In my faith and in my doubts
In my often weak efforts at holiness lived and nurtured
In my brokenness and woundedness
In my feelings of guilt and anger and fear. . .
Peace, be my healing.

In my actions and reactions
In my thoughts and moods and feelings
In my need to be accepted and loved
In my conversations with my sisters and my brothers
In my sincere attempts at reconciliation
In my spiritual journeying. . .
Peace, befriend me.

In both my successes and my failures
In my busyness and in my quiet
In my decisions and discernments
In my projects and endeavors
In my work and my leisure. . .
Peace, claim me.

Journal Suggestion

Begin your journal writing time with *John 14:24–28*.
Non-violence is the flower of peace. Do I acknowledge
the violence in my own heart: harsh words, a judgmental
attitude, unforgiveness, etc.? Am I a peacemaker? Do I see
this as part of my ministry as a Christian? Do I accept the
peace Jesus offers to me or do I look for it elsewhere?

Scripture Reading

John 14:24–28

Whoever does not love me does not keep my words; yet the
word you hear is not mine but that of the Father who sent me.
I have told you this while I am with you. The Advocate, the holy
Spirit that the Father will send in my name—he will teach you everything and remind you of all that [I] told you. Peace I leave with you;
my peace I give to you. Not as the world gives do I give it to you.
Do not let your hearts be troubled or afraid.

Your Journal Space

The Edge

How were you feeling, Jesus,
as you stood there alone before Pilate?
What were your thoughts?
Did you have **any** thoughts,
as you dangled there on the edge
between life and death?
Or were you overcome instead
with intense feelings?
...feelings of indescribable fear?
...feelings of justifiable anger?
...of rejection, loneliness, helplessness?
Had the feelings themselves
become the enemy for a time?
Were you discouraged with all
that you could yet accomplish;
had your hour not yet come?
Did you feel that all your teaching
and preaching,
all your miracles and cures
had been done in vain?

Jesus, I have read about
that night many times,
that shameful night
when God was put on trial,
that immemorial time in our history
when we condemned God
to death row.
Images of your silence
in the face of accusations,
your dignity in the face of Pilate,
have come to us through the ages.

But, inside, LORD—
what about inside?
Did you, at least for a moment,
wonder if it was all worth it?
Did you, in your humanness,
fall into a state of denial,
because the horror
of such brutal suffering
seemed so unbearable?

Was your silence
more of a paralysis,
a result of chronic shock,
a numbness one feels
when clinging to the edge,
with all the powers of evil
behind you, and a
seemingly bottomless pit before you?
Was the experience of incredible hurt
and absolute loss so unthinkable,
that it even became "unfeelable"?

If so, Jesus,
I feel much closer to you
than ever before.
My heart can really rest in yours,
with no need for embarrassment.
For, when you look into my eyes
and see all the feelings I have ever felt,
all the thoughts I have ever thought,
when I found myself on the edge
between life and death,
...joy and pain,
...sanity and chaos,
...charity and hatred.
When you see me there, LORD,
you really **do** understand,
and maybe even love me more.

Jesus, no matter how I try to hide
the unacceptable in me,
I really long for your love,
and I am grateful
for your healing hold on me.
May your name be praised forevermore!

Journal Suggestion

Begin your journal writing time by reading and reflecting on
Philippians 2:6–11. "The Edge" came to birth from reflection on
the first Station: "Jesus Is Condemned to Death." Choose any of
the traditional Stations or a Scripture scene from accounts of Jesus'
Passion, and speak to Jesus. Perhaps, you would like to carry it one
step further, and give Jesus time to respond to you. Write out your
dialogue in the journal space.

Scripture Reading

Philippians 2:6–11

Who, though he was in the form of God,
did not regard equality with God
    something to be grasped.
    Rather, he emptied himself,
taking the form of a slave,
coming in human likeness;
and found human in appearance,
    he humbled himself,
becoming obedient to death,
    even death on a cross.
Because of this, God greatly exalted him
and bestowed on him the name
that is above every name,
    that at the name of Jesus
every knee should bend,
of those in heaven and on earth and under
    the earth,
    and every tongue confess that
Jesus Christ is Lord,
to the glory of God the Father.

Your Journal Space

Simon Peter Returns

Forgive my intrusion.
I have come to share.
I have come to tell you
the lesson of love
I have learned from Jesus.
    My name is Simon Peter.
    I am closer to you than you know.
    The lesson I share is threefold.
    I speak of my cross, my grace,
    and my identity.

        My cross is not what you think.
        It is not the cross on which
        I was nailed for love of Him,
        the one that turned my world upside down
        because of my unworthiness.
        It is not even the Cross,
        the Sacred Cross on which
        my LORD and Savior was nailed,
        the Holy Wood
        that is our Salvation and Story.
            No, the cross that I carry even today,
            the cross that I thought would kill me,
            and, at times, I wished would have killed me,
            is only a memory,
            the memory of the day I denied Jesus.
            Oh, whenever I think of that dreadful night,
            my heart aches with sorrow and pain.
            At one time, I was overcome
            with guilt and shame.
            The emptiness within my spirit
            was a hole carved out by the
            sword of disappointment in my self
            and the curse of self-hatred.
                I loved Jesus so much...
                more than I could ever conceive.
                I just didn't understand.
                Was my fear even greater than my love?
                Were three years of faithfulness and friendship,
                three years of unbelievable graces,
                reduced to a mere sham
                in the span of just moments?

Every word Jesus spoke
was embedded in the depths of my heart,
where, like Mary, I pondered it,
and treasured it as gift.
Each time our eyes met,
something within me stirred
and leaped for joy,
as it had once happened to Elizabeth.
Like Samuel, like Isaiah,
I have often proclaimed,
"Speak, LORD, Your servant is listening."
"Here I am, LORD."
"Send me, LORD."
Perhaps my being chosen by Jesus
made me too confident
in the loyalty I felt.
Perhaps, I had forgotten for a while
that all that I had and all that I am
are due only to the graciousness
and giftedness of God.

> Yes, I cannot deny the truth,
> as I had once denied my God.
> It **had** happened.
> I really did not believe Jesus's prediction:
> "I tell you solemnly, Simon,
> before the cock crows,
> you will have denied me three times."
> These words had virtually stunned me.
> But, it really happened.
> In the face of danger,
> in the face of frightening oppression,
> in the face of evil itself,
> I, the friend and confidante,
> I, the chosen disciple,
> had—not once, but three times—
> disowned Jesus.
> I had failed him.
> I had let down my best friend.

This is my cross, my friends.
I carry it always.
I cannot change history.

My grace, however,
is greater than my cross.
I had shed countless tears
with my brothers
over the death of Jesus,
over the way they treated Him,
over the excruciating pain,
the tearing apart of His body,
and the open wound
of abandonment and rejection
that cut into his Sacred Heart.
I wept bitterly, too, for our loss;
for, we missed him so!
But...it was in the privacy of night
that I cried...
sobbed uncontrollably at times,
over my sin,
over my denial of Jesus.
My shame was so unbearable,
that I thought I could never look
into his eyes again.
Then, something wonderful happened.
Once, when Jesus came to us,
after that glorious Resurrection morning,
Jesus took me aside
and changed my life.
He asked me three times
if I loved him.
At first I was puzzled.
Jesus knew me.
He knew my love for him,
as clearly as he had known
my approaching denials.
Yet, Jesus kept asking me
if I loved him.
Each time I answered
"Yes, LORD You **know** that I love You."

And as those words left my lips,
I could feel, literally feel,
the scars of self-condemnation heal.
I could feel myself becoming whole again.
And when he told me,
"Feed my lambs...Feed my sheep,"
I knew—really knew
the glory of the Cross,
the compassion and forgiveness
of a loving God.
This is my grace.
    I had become the forgiven prodigal Son.
    I had become the healed paralytic.
    I had become the changed adulterous woman,
    the blind man,
    the leper,
    the one possessed,
    the prostitute...
I, who had been marked by shame
had now been saved by love.
I had been healed, strengthened, forgiven,
and—most surprising of all—
I, unworthy and undeserving servant,
had been **chosen again** by Jesus,
to lead his Church.
This is my grace, my friends,
the tender mercy and compassion of Jesus.

      There is one more lesson—my identity.
      You see, I am more than Simon Peter.
      I am you...and you...and you.
      Don't be afraid to look inside
      and find me there—
      the one who has denied Jesus—
      the person who has put other things
          in life before Him—
      the one who has yielded
      to the power of fear—
      who was lacking in trust—
      the person inside of you who is afraid
          to look into the eyes of Jesus.

Don't be afraid, Simon Peter!
Jesus forgives you.
He loves you still.
He loves you in your weakness.
You can be a fitting instrument
of Jesus's power,
as I am.
Listen for his voice.
He is calling you aside,
and speaking to your heart.
Answer him.
Your answer itself will free you.
"Simon Peter, do you love me?"

Journal Suggestion

Read the Scripture passage *John 21:15–19*, and then reread the poem. Can you sit in the stillness and let the Simon Peter within you come forth? Let Jesus heal the brokenness of past mistakes and weaknesses, as he did for Peter. When you are ready, write down what you feel has been your cross, your grace, and your identity.

Scripture Reading

John 21:15–19

When they had finished breakfast, Jesus said to Simon Peter, "Simon, son of John, do you love me more than these?" He said to him, "Yes, Lord, you know that I love you." He said to him, "Feed my lambs." He then said to him a second time, "Simon, son of John, do you love me?" He said to him, "Yes, Lord, you know that I love you." He said to him, "Tend my sheep." He said to him the third time, "Simon, son of John, do you love me?" Peter was distressed that he had said to him a third time, "Do you love me?" and he said to him, "Lord, you know everything; you know that I love you." [Jesus] said to him, "Feed my sheep. Amen, amen, I say to you, when you were younger, you used to dress yourself and go where you wanted; but when you grow old, you will stretch out your hands, and someone else will dress you and lead you where you do not want to go." He said this signifying by what kind of death he would glorify God. And when he had said this, he said to him, "Follow me."

Your Journal Space

Autumn Lessons from a Midnight Friend

The world around me sleeps
and I am here with Jesus.
The invitation?
"Stay awake with me;
watch and pray,
that you do not enter into temptation."
It seems—tonight—
I am hearing it for the first time.
It awakens me
from a sleep of my own choosing.

Daytime diversions
have their hypnotic power.
Unknowingly,
I walk through the day
in a make-shift trance—
a world of entertainment,
a world where nothing is real,
and reality is ignored.
Walt Disney Productions,
Warner Brothers films,
even Danielle Steel...
These are not evil—
only empty...
empty places
that pull us in
and divert our attentions
from a life fully lived.

But, in the peace
of night-time solitude,
I can see truth,
all that is real,
all that is constant,
in the depths of our existence.
You see,
nature is a dynamic teacher,
'tho I seldom give her
my listening ear.
Even now,
at the midnight hour,
I look out at the leaves,

playfully scattered
across our grounds,
their colors displaying
the whole spectrum
of Autumn beauty.
I look at the trees,
not quite so elaborately dressed,
as they were last April.
I hear the wind,
whistling its way
through branches and bushes—
creating a dance-like response
to the music it plays.

Fall is in the air.
And as I witness its signs,
as I touch it and smell it,
feel it and breathe it in,
I think about dying and rising,
shedding and new births,
letting go,
and trusting in fertile seeds,
submitting to the flow of the cosmos
with hope in the promise
of future life renewed.

And I know
that I, too, must do my homework,
and learn my lesson well.
I, too, must shed some
and die some.
I, too, must let go
and submit to the grace
of God's mysterious ways.

Oh yes, there is so much to see
here in the dark.
All looks really clear
at the sound
of the clock's midnight chime.
Little by little,
I will attune myself
to this realm of life—
even in the daytime.
For, midnight is not merely a time,
but also a place.
I must find some midnight places
in my life.

It is there
that I can truly meet Jesus,
the LORD of all our risings
and new births,
the God of timelessness
and infinite space.
Wake me up, Jesus.

Jesus, call me to see
the dawning of a new day
in the deep recesses of my heart.
Bid me to walk with you,
my night-time friend...
hand-in-hand,
day or night...
the road of abundant life,
even if it is
the one less travelled.

Journal Suggestion

Read and reflect on *Psalm 139*. Does the poem and scripture
reading inspire some response from you? Try writing your
thoughts in the journal space. Do you, too, need to find
some "midnight places" in your life? Spend time with your
"Midnight Friend," and afterwards, journal your experience.

Scripture Reading

Psalm 139
The All-knowing and Ever-present God
1 For the leader. A psalm of David.

I

LORD, you have probed me, you know me:
    you know when I sit and stand;
    you understand my thoughts from afar.
My travels and my rest you mark;
    with all my ways you are familiar.
Even before a word is on my tongue,
    LORD, you know it all.
Behind and before you encircle me
    and rest your hand upon me.
Such knowledge is beyond me,
    far too lofty for me to reach.

II

Where can I hide from your spirit?
    From your presence, where can I flee?
If I ascend to the heavens, you are there;
    if I lie down in Sheol, you are there too.
If I fly with the wings of dawn
    and alight beyond the sea,
Even there your hand will guide me,
    your right hand hold me fast.
If I say, "Surely darkness shall hide me,
    and night shall be my light"—
Darkness is not dark for you,
    and night shines as the day.
    Darkness and light are but one.

III

You formed my inmost being;
    you knit me in my mother's womb.
I praise you, so wonderfully you made me;
    wonderful are your works!
My very self you knew;
    my bones were not hidden from you,
When I was being made in secret,
    fashioned as in the depths of the earth.

Your Journal Space

Rediscovering My Heart

What Is a Christian Heart?

A Christian heart
is a heart that feels
all that there is to feel,
without fear or hesitation.
It knows that in feeling deeply
one enters into the fullness
of what it means to be human
and becomes most fully
sister or brother
to all of humanity.

A Christian heart
sees clearly
because it rejects all choices
that would block vision.
All the world is a painting,
and the Artist Himself
can be seen in the masterpiece
if one looks at the whole,
no matter what it asks,
no matter the cost.

A Christian heart
is one that **is.**
It **becomes** all that it feels,
so that its sensitivity
can call others to feel too,
to feel for their sisters and brothers,
to feel with them.
It **becomes** all that it sees,
both the joys and the pains,
both the longings and the sorrows,
so that it can **be** all things
to all people.

A Christian heart
in its feeling,
in its seeing,
in its becoming,
indeed in its very being,
is a lover and a maker,
a lover of peace,
a maker of peace,
among all of God's people,
throughout all of the earth.

Journal Suggestion

The surest way to get to the "heart of the matter"—particularly, into your own heart—is through the heart of God. Take some time with *Matthew 11:28–30*. Picture Jesus sitting with you, as He invites you to "come" to Him and tells you of His gentle heart. Ask Him to guide you on your heart journey. After spending some time with this imaging, write down your experiences, feelings, and reactions.

Scripture Reading

Matthew 11:28–30

"Come to me, all you who labor and are burdened, and I will give you rest. Take my yoke upon you and learn from me, for I am meek and humble of heart, and you will find rest for yourselves. For my yoke is easy, and my burden light."

Your Journal Space

Part III

Living the
Paschal Mystery

Beatitudes Alive

Blessed are those who, like the saints of old,
have heard my call deep in their hearts
and have responded with full hearts and willing spirits;
for, theirs is the kingdom of God.

Blessed are those who have dedicated their lives to me,
and who have made that dedication a real part of their everyday living;
for, they shall inherit the earth.

Blessed are those who, like the first century Christians,
love one another not only in word, but with every fiber of their being—
living, working, praying always in communion with each other;
for, they shall see God.

Blessed are those who value unity more than their own opinions
and respect for another more than their own needs;
for, they shall always have my blessing.

Blessed are those who are open to the new ways of the Spirit in their lives,
but also wise enough to value tradition and history;
for, they shall be filled with my graces.

Blessed are those who can make new beginnings
with freshness of mind and eagerness in their steps;
for, they shall be free.

Blessed are those who are not afraid to grieve
during times of transition, to feel during times of loss,
and to choose healing and new life for themselves and others;
for, they shall receive a hundredfold.

Blessed are those who, in the spirit of **today's** saints,
pray faithfully, who serve untiringly,
and who say a hearty "yes" to every invitation from their God;
for, theirs is the kingdom of God.

Journal Suggestion:

Reflecting on the Beatitudes in *Matthew 5:1–12*, write your own "blessings." Then, let *Ephesians 4:1–6* challenge you to use your blessing as an examination of conscience. Choose the beatitude that you need to work on more attentively right now. Write it down in your journal space with some concrete ways that can help you to take some definite steps in that area.

Scripture Readings

Matthew 5:1–12

The Sermon on the Mount
When he saw the crowds, he went up the mountain, and after he had sat down, his disciples came to him. He began to teach them, saying:

The Beatitudes
Blessed are the poor in spirit,
for theirs is the kingdom of heaven.
Blessed are they who mourn,
for they will be comforted.
Blessed are the meek,
for they will inherit the land.
Blessed are they who hunger and thirst for
righteousness,
for they will be satisfied.
Blessed are the merciful,
for they will be shown mercy.
Blessed are the clean of heart,
for they will see God.
Blessed are the peacemakers,
for they will be called children of God.
Blessed are they who are persecuted for
the sake of righteousness,
for theirs is the kingdom of heaven.

Blessed are you when they insult you and persecute you and utter every kind of evil against you [falsely] because of me. Rejoice and be glad, for your reward will be great in heaven. Thus they persecuted the prophets who were before you.

Ephesians 4:1–6

I, then, a prisoner for the Lord, urge you to live in a manner worthy of the call you have received, with all humility and gentleness, with patience, bearing with one another through love, striving to preserve the unity of the spirit through the bond of peace: one body and one Spirit, as you were also called to the one hope of your call; one Lord, one faith, one baptism; one God and Father of all, who is over all and through all and in all.

Your Journal Space

Hope Restored

A new city
Augustine's "City of God,"
Jerusalem reborn
A new world order,
A place of freedom
    of liberation and justice;
A place of the heart
    where the powerful are loved into healing
    where oppressors no longer have need to rule;
A place where dignity and respect,
    reverence and harmony
    all make their home
and only those who value their presence
    are welcome.

Does such a city really exist?
Or is it only some dream,
    some saving fantasy
    in a desperate mind full of unrest?
The God humanity
    calls us to build this city
    to build steadily and faithfully
    until the journey's end.
With hope, we will proclaim
—perhaps, with arms stretched out on a cross—
"It is finished."

Journal Suggestion

Read *I Peter 2:4–6*. You are a "living stone"! Stones can be used to either build up or to destroy. Do you "build" through your actions? your words? Are there times your actions or words bring destruction?

Scripture Reading

I Peter 2:4–6

Come to him, a living stone, rejected by human beings but
chosen and precious in the sight of God, and, like living stones,
let yourselves be built into a spiritual house to be a holy priesthood
to offer spiritual sacrifices acceptable to God through Jesus Christ.
For it says in scripture:

> "Behold, I am laying a stone in Zion,
>   a cornerstone, chosen and precious,
> and whoever believes in it shall not be
>   put to shame."

Your Journal Space

Tent People

We are tent people.
Our spiritual roots testify to this.
We read of the tents
    of Abraham and Sarah,
    of Isaac and Rebekah.
We know that Paul was
    a tentmaker by trade,
    and because of his travels,
    he often slept in one himself.

We are tent people—
    wandering nomads
    on the move,
    always on the move,
    settling in wherever the need is,
    but also ready
    at a moment's call,
    at a sign of change
    in the direction of the wind,
    to fold up our tents
    and go to the place
    where we are sent,
    to do the work of Yahweh,
    as did the judges and prophets
    of our history.

Like Samuel, disciple of Eli,
Like Isaiah with lips seared and cleansed,
Like Jeremiah
    with God's handprint on his mouth,
    we fall on our knees again and again
    and proclaim
    with hearts of faith and courage
    our "Here I am, LORD."

For tent people,
    life means movement
    Joy is found in the journey itself,
    because we walk together.
    And, as we go, we praise our God.
Like Moses' times,
    our tents are "tents of meeting"
    where God's dwelling rests.
    And herein in our peace!
    Wherever we go...
    "I will be with you always,
    even until the end of time."

Journal Suggestion

Read *Genesis 13:14–18*. For Abraham, every time he responded to the voice of God it meant movement. "He picked up his tent—." Each move was a graced moment. Perhaps God is not asking you to move in a literal sense but God does expect movement in our spiritual life. Do I carry a status quo mentality or am I open to change? Am I too comfortable in my secure work to risk the insecurities of the pilgrim world? What does "folding up your tent and moving" mean for you right now in your spiritual journey?

Scripture Reading

Genesis 13:14–18

After Lot had left, the Lord said to Abram: "Look about you, and from where you are, gaze to the north and south, east and west; all the land that you see I will give to you and your descendants forever. I will make your descendants like the dust of the earth; if anyone could count the dust of the earth, your descendants too might be counted. Set forth and walk about in the land, through its length and breadth, for to you I will give it." Abram moved his tents and went on to settle near the terebinth of Mamre, which is at Hebron. There he built an altar to the Lord.

Your Journal Space

Women of God

Women of God,
    saints of our roots,
    you stand in history as symbols,
    as paragons of faith.
    Though you surely must have felt
    the degrading injustice
    toward women of your time,
    you now radiate
    dignity and grace,
    a distinctive feature
    of God's holy ones.
    Yes, you are our models,
    our teachers, our mentors,
    our emblems of victory
    and glory.
    We praise God for you.

Woman at the well,
    You have been touched,
    forgiven, and loved by Jesus.
    Your past healed,
    your future opened,
    you faced your God in truth
    and learned
    how healing and freeing it is
    to be known.
    We praise God for you.

Woman caught in adultery,
    How fearful you must have felt,
    as you were thrown into the center
    of the violent crowd.
    Did you ever think
    that you would have been treated
    with such compassion,
    such understanding?
    The gracious forgiveness
    and mercy are indeed
    signs of how God loved you.
    We praise God for you.

Woman with the hemorrhage,
    What joy you must have felt
    in your heart!
    For the first time in twelve years,
    a serge of healing and new life
    filled your body.
    Surely, your soul, too,
    must have been changed!
    Gratitude must have taken over
    your abused heart,
    and a feeling of awe
    overcome your tired spirit.
    We praise God for you.

Woman who anointed the feet of Jesus,
    So humble, so simple, so unafraid!
    You felt the power,
    and let yourself be drawn to Jesus
    in the embrace of freedom
    and the truth of repentance.
    Oh, how you loved Jesus
    Who first loved you!
    We praise God for you.

Woman, mother of God,
    Woman of all women,
    you are a model of faith for us.
    You had the openness
    to hear an angel,
    the courage
    to say "Yes" to your God
    even in the midst of
    judgment and danger,
    and the wisdom "to ponder
    all these things in your heart."
    Whether you found yourself
    at the stable crib,
    or the passion cross,
    at the holy city temple,
    or the Cana wedding,
    your relationship
    with Jesus,
    was shown to be
    intimate and faithful.
    We praise God for you.

Women of God,
  hold your heads high
  as you take your place
  among the chosen of God,
  the Communion of Saints.
  Do you not realize that
  all who find themselves
  on the margins,
  all who are unacceptable
  to the powerful,
  and to the "culturally correct,"
  see in you the Rising Sun
  on the distant, but visible, horizon?
  We praise God for you.
  It is of you that Jesus said,
  "Blessed are the poor in spirit;
  the kingdom of heaven is theirs."

Journal Suggestion

Read *Luke 1:46–56.* Mary magnified the LORD. She recognized God's work in her. She, the lowly one, the marginal, had been lifted up, had been exalted. This she knew of her God, who cared so much for those on the edges of society. Have you ever felt put down, oppressed by others, their expectations? What were your feelings at those times? Did you turn to God to be lifted up or did you allow the oppressor to keep you down? Do you reach out to those on the "edges of society"? Write your own Magnificat. End your journal writing time by praying Mary's Magnificat.

Scripture Reading

Luke 1:46–56

The Canticle of Mary. And Mary said:
"My soul proclaims the greatness of the
Lord;
my spirit rejoices in God my savior.
For he has looked upon his handmaid's
lowliness;
behold, from now on will all ages call
me blessed.
The Mighty One has done great things
for me,
and holy is his name.
His mercy is from age to age
to those who fear him.
He has shown might with his arm,
dispersed the arrogant of mind and
heart.
He has thrown down the rulers from
their thrones
but lifted up the lowly.
The hungry he has filled with good
things;
the rich he has sent away empty.
He has helped Israel his servant,
remembering his mercy,
according to his promise to our fathers,
to Abraham and to his descendants
forever."

Mary remained with her about three months and then returned home.

Your Journal Space

A Toast

Life,
you have many faces,
many yet unseen.
My search must go on.
I seek you always.
Wherever we have met,
there also was my God.

Life, I choose you.
And I commit myself
to the God of life,
to the God Who offers me your fullness,
to the God of wholeness,
of healing,
of vibrant joy.

Life,
I choose you,
because to be fully alive
is to be committed to truth,
and the truth *will* set me free.

But what is truth?
Not like Pilate, do we ask,
condemning, frightened Pilate,
but as disciples,
longing,
yearning
for more of you.

Isn't truth wherever
we find ourselves,
wherever we find
our sisters and brothers?
Isn't truth right there
in our hearts,
feeling our feelings?
...grieving our losses?
...celebrating our joys?

Yes, life,
I choose you,
not in the aesthetic beauty
of pious words,
nor in the idealistic picture
of "someday" dreams.
I choose you here.
I choose you now,
in this particular home in which I live,
with the particular people who now
work with me,
eat with me,
pray and play with me.

Life,
you who do not dwell in some
"never-never-land-Utopia,"
you who are real,
ancient but ever so new,
concrete yet full of surprises,
I find you in the depths,
but also in the heights.
And I choose you.

To you, life,
I raise a toast.
I drink this wine,
this transforming Cana wine
in your honor.
I celebrate you.
I rejoice in your presence
within me
and around me.

May this wine,
symbolic of the blood of Jesus,
my love and my life,
become a living part of me.
May it pour itself out,
birthing life into all I touch.

Amen.

Journal Suggestion

Pray with *Deuteronomy 30:15-20.* "I place before you life and death. Choose life." List choices you made in the past that were life-giving. Name the good that came from them. List choices you made that were not life-giving. How did they hinder your growth? Continue the lists below, drawing from your own experiences:

To choose life means	To choose death means
To forgive	To hold resentment
To accept change	To resist change
To live in the "now"	To live in the past
To love unconditionally	To love conditionally
To love	To hate
To see good	To concentrate on faults
To risk	To play it safe
To acknowledge limitations	To deny limitations

Scripture Reading

Deuteronomy 30:15-20

The Choice before Israel. "Here, then, I have today set before you life and prosperity, death and doom. If you obey the commandments of the LORD, your God, which I enjoin on you today, loving him, and walking in his ways, and keeping his commandments, statutes and decrees, you will live and grow numerous, and the LORD, your God, will bless you in the land you are entering to occupy. If, however, you turn away your hearts and will not listen, but are led astray and adore and serve other gods, I tell you now that you will certainly perish; you will not have a long life on the land which you are crossing the Jordan to enter and occupy. I call heaven and earth today to witness against you. I have set before you life and death, the blessing and the curse. Choose life, then, that you and your descendants may live, by loving the LORD, your God, heeding his voice, and holding fast to him. For that will mean life for you, a long life for you to live on the land which the LORD swore he would give to your fathers Abraham and Jacob."

Your Journal Space

Called to Servanthood

Have you washed any feet lately?
Not faces, not hands! Feet!
Dirty feet,
soiled from a long day's travels.
Do it in the name of Jesus.

Have you reached out
to your sister or brother lately?
The ones whose gaits
are slow and irregular?
Years of service
have distorted their feet
and left them limp.
Hold them up
in the name of Jesus.

Have you been a footwasher
to the people you serve?
To the "least" of them?
They too need to feel
the love of Jesus,
the respect that
human dignity allows them.
Kneel down before them,
and wash their feet
in the name of Jesus.

Have you yourself
received from *you*
the love and affection
that you give to others?
Bow down
before the mystery of *you*.
Be a footwasher to yourself
in the name of Jesus.

Journal Suggestion

Read *John 13:1–9*. Reflect on this passage and then read the poem again. Whom do you consider "the least"? Try to image in your mind washing the feet of someone you put in your "least" group. Note your feelings as you wash. How does he/she seem to react? Now, hand them the water basin and towel and let them wash *your* feet. How do you feel as the receiver of the service? Has your concept of "the least" changed?

Scripture Reading

John 13:1–9

The Washing of the Disciples' Feet

Before the feast of Passover, Jesus knew that his hour had come to pass from this world to the Father. He loved his own in the world and he loved them to the end. The devil had already induced Judas, son of Simon the Iscariot, to hand him over. So, during supper, fully aware that the Father had put everything into his power and that he had come from God and was returning to God, he rose from supper and took off his outer garments. He took a towel and tied it around his waist. Then he poured water into a basin and began to wash the disciples' feet and dry them with the towel around his waist. He came to Simon Peter, who said to him, "Master, are you going to wash my feet?" Jesus answered and said to him, "What I am doing, you do not understand now, but you will understand later." Peter said to him, "You will never wash my feet." Jesus answered him, "Unless I wash you, you will have no inheritance with me." Simon Peter said to him, "Master, then not only my feet, but my hands and head as well."

Your Journal Space

The Circle of Life

What is a circle?
Those who opened their ears to the message of Paul
and their hearts to Jesus whom he preached,
were drawn into the circle.
They could form circles only because
they were already a part
of the circle of life.

What is a circle?
I see the followers of Paul *before* any time of danger,
encircled around him,
pulled to him by the dynamism
of his faith,
of his words,
of the Spirit alive in him.
Unknowingly, they are lured into that same Spirit,
and there, became one in mind and heart,

What is a circle?
Jesus in the temple,
the Wisdom of God in the body of a young boy!
There in the center...
Jesus encircled...
He teaches and guides and reveals the Father's love
The priests, the leaders, the elders surround Jesus
in a shared spirit of wonder and awe.
Jesus on a mountain, in a boat,
on the shore, even at the market place—
the focus of encircled life!
The numbers seem countless;
the needs, endless—
all coming to the circle
to be healed, to be taught,
ultimately to be loved.

What is a circle?
It is the disciples of "the Way."
It is the Body of Christ
in *this* age, in *this* place
gathered around our *center*,
Jesus the Christ.
It is all who are of one mind and one heart,
those who sing with one voice
and live in love and charity.
*"This is how they will know
that you are my disciples:
that you have love for one another."*

Journal Suggestion

1. Read *Acts 4:32–35*. Think of some of the circles of which you are a part—*e.g.*, your family circle, your circle of friends, a circle of coworkers... Take each of these circles of people in your life, and place each person in them before the LORD Jesus for a special blessing. Then, pray for yourself. Ask Jesus to draw you more deeply into his circle of intimate friends. Write your prayer freely, as your longing for intimacy with Jesus comes to the foreground.

2. If you are a person who can look in retrospect on your life this far, and see some conflicting, interlocking circles in which you seem to have been trapped for some time, perhaps this is also a good time to gently call those circles forth. Place those circles, too, before your loving God, and ask for any necessary healing. As you do this remembering, can you now see some good in those circles that you couldn't see at the time?

Scripture Readings

Acts 4:32–35

Life in the Christian Community

The community of believers was of one heart and mind, and no one claimed that any of his possessions was his own, but they had everything in common. With great power the apostles bore witness to the resurrection of the Lord Jesus, and great favor was accorded them all. There was no needy person among them, for those who owned property or houses would sell them, bring the proceeds of the sale, and put them at the feet of the apostles, and they were distributed to each according to need.

Acts 14:19–22

However, some Jews from Antioch and Iconium arrived and won over the crowds. They stoned Paul and dragged him out of the city, supposing that he was dead. But when the disciples gathered around him, he got up and entered the city. On the following day he left with Barnabas for Derbe.

After they had proclaimed the good news to that city and made a considerable number of disciples, they returned to Lystra and to Iconium and to Antioch. They strengthened the spirits of the disciples and exhorted them to persevere in the faith, saying, "It is necessary for us to undergo many hardships to enter the kingdom of God."

Your Journal Space

Abba, Father

(Our Father—adapted)

Abba, Father,
You who live in the heavens of my heart,
Holy and awesome is your name!
Each whispering of it
fills me with grace and life,
strengthening and empowering me.
Abba, be my King,
and teach me how to serve you.
May all my time,
my energies, my gifts,
be spent on pleasing You.
Glory to You, Abba,
here and in all places,
now and in all times.
Feed and nurture me, O God.
Nourish me for each day's work,
done in honor of your kingship.

Loving, compassionate God.
Gentle me, tender me,
so that I may be softly accepting of others.
Only then can I come to You, Abba,
humbly hoping that my hardness,
my sinful thoughts and actions
draw only Your mercy and love.
Abba, you know how weak I can be,
how easily I fall back
in my daily journey forward.
Free me from my most difficult obstacle,
my own self.
May Your name, "Abba," be always
the prayer on my lips
and the life of my soul.

Amen.

Journal Suggestion

After reflecting on the Our Father, the Scripture text from *Romans 8:14–17*, and *Psalm 103*, try writing your own "Our Father."

Scripture Readings

Romans 8:14–17

For those who are led by the Spirit of God are children of God. For you did not receive a spirit of slavery to fall back into fear, but you received a spirit of adoption, through which we cry, "*Abba*, Father!" The Spirit itself bears witness with our spirit that we are children of God, and if children, then heirs, heirs of God and joint heirs with Christ, if only we suffer with him so that we may also be glorified with him.

Psalm 103

Praise of Divine Goodness
1 of David
I
Bless the LORD, my soul;
    all my being, bless his holy name!
Bless the LORD, my soul;
    do not forget all the gifts of God,
Who pardons all your sins,
    heals all your ills,
Delivers your life from the pit,
    surrounds you with love and compassion,
Fills your days with good things;
    your youth is renewed like the eagle's.

II
The LORD does righteous deeds,
    brings justice to all the oppressed.
His ways were revealed to Moses,
    mighty deeds to the people of Israel.
Merciful and gracious is the LORD,
    slow to anger, abounding in kindness.
God does not always rebuke,
    nurses no lasting anger,
Has not dealt with us as our sins merit,
    nor requited us as our deeds deserve.

III

As the heavens tower over the earth,
    so God's love towers over the faithful.
As far as the east is from the west,
    so far have our sins been removed from
        us.
As a father has compassion on his children,
    so the LORD has compassion on the
        faithful.
For he knows how we are formed,
    remembers that we are dust.
Our days are like the grass;
    like flowers of the field we blossom.
The wind sweeps over us and we are gone;
    our place knows us no more.
But the LORD's kindness is forever,
    toward the faithful from age to age.
He favors the children's children
    of those who keep his covenant,
    who take care to fulfill its precepts.

IV

The LORD's throne is established in heaven;
    God's royal power rules over all.
Bless the LORD, all you angels,
    might in strength and attentive,
    obedient to every command.
Bless the LORD, all you hosts,
    ministers who do God's will.
Bless the LORD, all creatures,
    everywhere in God's domain.
Bless the LORD, my soul!

Your Journal Space

Transfigured God

Eucharistic God
transfigured before me
on the altar.
What gift!
You have not limited
the sharing of your glory
to Peter, James, and John,
but...are here before our eyes.
All we need do is
to look...and believe.

On Tabor Mountain
Your three friends
saw brilliance,
a glimpse of Divinity—
your robes dazzling
as bright as a blanket of snow
reflecting in the glow
of the rising sun.
On this mountain,
this holy place
of your Eucharistic presence,
I see the depths of humanity.
I see bread for hungry people,
your people,
hungry for love and forgiveness,
hungry for healing,
for new life,
hungry for hearts full of peace.
I see the Bread of Life
for people who know
that you are their God.
When I look upon this deified host,
I see, too,
those who hunger for food,
the poor, the oppressed,
the sick, the lonely,
the grieving, the abused.
They too are a part of your body,
that is held up before me
with consecrated hands,
to consume, to absorb
into my heart and spirit.

Peter, James, and John
were graced with the vision
of Moses and Elijah.
I do not see these ancient forefathers
on my Eucharistic mountain.
I look at transformed bread,
and see my sisters and brothers.
I see all who have come
to Your supper.
I turn to them
with my more-than-ritual sign of peace,
and look into their eyes,
No!—past their eyes—
into their souls,
and see my transfigured LORD there too.
I look all around me—
on my right side,
on my left,
before me and behind me,
and know with unwavering certainty
that *this* is the Body of Christ.

Peter knew the peace,
the intimacy he felt there.
"Let us build three tents, LORD,
one for You, one for Moses,
and one for Elijah."
Tents of worship,
dwelling places for the Holy Ones.
Oh, Peter,
hadn't you yet learned
that you cannot hold onto Divinity,
close it in, tie it down.
There is no place in the Kingdom
for possessiveness.
Listen!
Do you hear the voice of Yahweh, your God?
"This is my beloved son...Listen to him."

Jesus,
Eucharistic God,
Bethlehem-manger-God,
Nazareth-carpenter-God,
Cana-miracle-God,
Galilee-preacher-God,
Jericho-healer-God,
Calvary-Crucified God,
Jerusalem-Risen God,
Emmaus-Glorified God,
I cannot build you
tents and temples.
I can only bow down in silence,
and carry you in my heart
throughout the day
with tabernacle-reverence—
grateful to have been touched
by so awesome a mystery
as the Transfiguration
(not so much the Tabor-glory,
as the miracle-happening
on our altar every day!)
How blessed I am
to be invited
with Peter, James, and John
to *this* mountain!
And even here,
two millennia later,
if I listen very intently,
I can hear a Voice
resounding from another realm,
"This is My beloved Son...
Listen to him."

Journal Suggestion

Read *Mark 9:2–8*. Then, read the poem again thoughtfully.
Do you have any immediate responses of your own? Choose
one section of the prayer or the scripture passage that is inviting
you or challenging you at this point in your life, and write down
your feelings and thoughts.

Scripture Reading

Mark 9:2–8

After six days Jesus took Peter, James, and John and led them up a high mountain apart by themselves. And he was transfigured before them, and his clothes became dazzling white, such as no fuller on earth could bleach them. Then Elijah appeared to them along with Moses, and they were conversing with Jesus. Then Peter said to Jesus in reply, "Rabbi, it is good that we are here! Let us make three tents: one for you, one for Moses, and one for Elijah." He hardly knew what to say, they were so terrified. Then a cloud came, casting a shadow over them; then from the cloud came a voice, "This is my beloved Son. Listen to him." Suddenly, looking around, they no longer saw anyone but Jesus alone with them.

Your Journal Space

Who Do You Say That I Am?

How easy to profess fidelity
while playing our idolatry games!
Rehoboams come into our lives,
setting up their temples and gods,
placing golden calves before us.
And, unaware,
as if in a trance of sleep,
we bow down in worship.
Our need for security,
our fears about the future,
our misconceptions about each other,
our drive to feel important,
our distorted sense of priorities...
So much within us
rules our minds,
determines how we think
and act,
and receives our allegiance
and adorations—
divinized and tabernacled.

Soon Jesus will look upon us
from the altar of sacrifice.
And He will be moved with pity
at how our hearts hunger
for what is real,
for what really satisfies
and nourishes.
He will take whatever loaves and fish
he can find among us.
He will hold all in his miracle hands,
breathe transforming life,
multiply,
and distribute.
He will feed us
as he has already fed our souls
with his words,
our whole beings with his presence.

Jesus becomes our focal point,
the desire of our common heart.
Drawn into the sacramental
experience of grace,
we become "Eucharisted" together.
Peace and joy,
forgiveness and love,
freedom and life renewed
overwhelm our spirits.
Too much food to digest!
Too little to fill completely
the hunger within!

A miracle happens
on our altars every day,
just as it happened to a
mountainside hungering crowd.
Each day we touch the sacred
in a timeless moment
of sacramental sharing.
Do we leave the sanctuary
affected and healed
and changed...forever?
Or do we return
down the mountain
to our daily schedules,
and drink our secular coffee,
ready to pay homage
to our golden calves?

Journal Suggestion

Read *John 6:1–15* and *Mark 8:27–30*. After reflecting on these passages, decide who Jesus is for you. How real is Jesus at the Eucharistic table, in the Liturgy of the Word? Is Jesus just as real in the celebrating assembly? After reflection, write *your* profession of faith.

Scripture Readings

John 6:1–15

Multiplication of the Loaves. After this, Jesus went across the Sea of Galilee [of Tiberias]. A large crowd followed him, because they saw the signs he was performing on the sick. Jesus went up on the mountain, and there he sat down with his disciples. The Jewish feast of Passover was near. When Jesus raised his eyes and saw that a large crowd was coming to him, he said to Philip, "Where can we buy enough food for them to eat?" He said this to test him, because he himself knew what he was going to do. Philip answered him, "Two hundred days' wages worth of food would not be enough for each of them to have a little [bit]." One of his disciples, Andrew, the brother of Simon Peter, said to him, "There is a boy here who has five barley loaves and two fish; but what good are these for so many?" Jesus said, "Have the people recline." Now there was a great deal of grass in that place. So the men reclined, about five thousand in number. Then Jesus took the loaves, gave thanks, and distributed them to those who were reclining, and also as much of the fish as they wanted. When they had had their fill, he said to his disciples, "Gather the fragments left over, so that nothing will be wasted." So they collected them, and filled twelve wicker baskets with fragments from the five barley loaves that had been more than they could eat. When the people saw the sign he had done, they said, "This is truly the Prophet, the one who is to come into the world." Since Jesus knew that they were going to come and carry him off to make him king, he withdrew again to the mountain alone.

Mark 8:27–30

Now Jesus and his disciples set out for the villages of Caesarea Philippi. Along the way he asked his disciples, "Who do people say that I am?" They said in reply, "John the Baptist, others Elijah, still others one of the prophets." And he asked them, "But who do you say that I am?" Peter said to him in reply, "You are the Messiah." Then he warned them not to tell anyone about him.

Your Journal Space

The Religion series is one of five series published by **The Center for Learning**, a nonprofit educational corporation established in 1970. In addition to the Religion series, Center publications include approximately 350 curriculum units in English/Language Arts, Novels/Dramas, Social Studies, and Interdisciplinary Biographies.

TAP® is the Center's trademark, describing its distinct network of more than three hundred master **T**eachers who **A**uthor and **P**ublish the popular curriculum units currently used in more than 30,000 public, private, and parochial schools around the world.

The Center's original and continued commitment to improve the quality of education extends beyond its publications. The Center also takes an active role in renewing educators as professionals through its Professional Development Department. In-service programs are available on all Center series. In addition, an annual Evergreen Workshop is a scholarship opportunity to gain hands-on experience in selecting, evaluating, and creating effective lessons. This is an excellent prelude to becoming a professional Center for Learning author.

As we serve a growing number of teachers, we welcome your input. Please send us your evaluations and suggestions so that we can serve you better.

For **editorial information**, please contact:
The Center for Learning
Administrative/Editorial Office
21590 Center Ridge Road
Rocky River, OH 44116
(216) 331-1404   •   FAX (216) 331-5414

For **ordering information or catalogs** of individual series, contact:
The Center for Learning
Shipping/Business Office
P.O. Box 910
Villa Maria, PA 16155
(800) 767-9090   •   (412) 964-8083
FAX (412) 964-8992